THE EXPEDITION

Self-Discovery and Exploration

RICHA THAKUR

Made with ❤ on the BookLeaf Publishing Platform
www.bookleafpub.in
www.bookleafpub.com

Dedication

This book is dedicated to the amazing beauty of life, the moments of courage, resilience and authenticity. To those who enjoy nature and its beauty, and to those who like science fiction and spy movies. I hope this collection inspires you, and that you have a great time reading it.

Preface

Life is full of different kinds of feelings and emotions. In this collection, I have tried to capture those moments be it joy, love, trust, compassion, gratitude, hope, contentment or admiration. We all experience these phases, but they cannot be described any better than in a poetry. So, I decided to write a collection of them.

Nature invites exploration, expeditions, and observation. It consists of beautiful places and awe-inspiring moments that guide us. The beauty is endless and can't be penned down on a few pages. But still, I made an effort to dive a little closer to our amazing nature with my writings.

Acknowledgements

I would like to express my deepest gratitude to my family and friends. This work would not have been possible without their unwavering encouragement and support. I am also thankful to my teachers, who introduced me to poetry and its power to connect. I have also been inspired by pop music videos and fiction novels and the tales they tell. I am honored to share my piece of writing with all the readers.

You Are a Star

You were born for a difference in the world,
You were born to light like a chandelier star.
You've got that damn thing in your heart,
You can be the antidote to the poison and your scars.

They'll say that you woke up from a bad dream,
And you're walking straight out of the bars.
They'll say that you are brainless,
And you've nothing in your jars.

They have never seen
How fast you race your cars,
When you're out there in the track,
How you made it to this stage,
From being a sheep and now called a star.

We are the stars,
Nobody is there to stop the cars.
We are the stars,
No, no bars are made to block our hours.
We are the stars,
We are the stars,
We are the stars.

There's no one,
No one in the world,
Who thought you'd be a star.
But you believed in yourself,
And that's why today,
You are a star.
You are a star,
You are a star.

Another beginner on the street,
She has a roar inside.
She's everything she eyes.
Every second she works,
Makes her a star.
She'll be called a star,
She'll be called a star,
She'll be called a star.

Undercover Agent

He was involved in disguises and false identities,
Staking out a building and looking for opportunities.
It was then when he had met Hana and her equivalents.
She was perspicacious and quite intelligent.

Thought he was an undercover agent.
His dad was killed in a brush pass incident.
Told his allies to him when had just joined.
Just like his father, he was the master of his craft and
very relevant.

He stood there with a pistol in his hand.
All the espionage had led him to kill this woman.
Hana surrendered but she also handed him few disks.
He was going to turn them over to his leads.

But he went through the disks just to be plausible.
What he saw was completely unpredictable.
His dad was killed by his own agency.
It was run by prominent figures; he then regretted his
own transparency.

His country's security was compromised.
He was actually working for the high profiles.

He now had no one to confide in and to take his side.
But he devised a plan to sabotage their plan nationwide.

He mailed the agency and deceived them into thinking
he was from a secret group.
He asked them to reveal their motives and their truth.
But they denied so he decrypted all their codes.
Sadly, he was killed by them just before the crowd
arrived,
Who then took the power from the agency and
Brought a change in the system and its integrity.

Going into the Wild

I have filled my bags.
I graduated from college this year.
I'm thrilled to tell you that
I am going away from civilization.
I am going into the wild.

Today, I set my feet where the water runs.
I know where I have to go, but the paths are uncertain.
I have been climbing mountains these days.
My hands have toughened through the wild's embrace.
I am going away from civilization.
I am going into the wild.

I have been hitchhiking a lot lately.
I have finally found a beautiful spot.
It's across the lakeside.
I have tried to build a cabin there.
I am going away from civilization.
I am going into the wild.

He Didn't Wait for Her to be Taken by You

For all the sacrifices he made,
For all the fights he faced,
Kept her away from all those hates.
He didn't wait for her to be taken by you.
He didn't wait for her to be taken by you.

From childhood, they were the best of friends.
They saw each other grow in every sense.
Tied the ribbon and held each other's hands,
Only to see her smile and twirl her in dance.
He didn't wait for her to be taken by you.
He didn't wait for her to be taken by you.

Why come over when it's just not over?
She feels for him,
and she has always been his queen.
They weren't just ready and prepared
For you to come over and take her hand.
He didn't wait for her to be taken by you.
He didn't wait for her to be taken by you.

On the day of marriage,
When her veil unveils,

She will stay there silent,
Cause all she will be thinking
Will be about the days
She spent,
Not with you but with him instead.
She didn't wait for her to be taken by you.
She didn't wait for her to be taken by you.

Now the battle that you have just won,
As her parents think that you are the one.
She will be called to have happily married,
No there is no pun.
Now you can take her, it is all done.

After years, he again sees her in the mall.
She now seems to be smiling above a beautiful shawl.
But this time, her smile belongs to you and not him, of
course.
He stands there smiling because now he has finally lost.
He didn't wait for her to be taken by you.
He didn't wait for her to be taken by you.

Humankind and Masterminds

There were inventions and inceptions,
Got to be revolutionary conceptions,
Developed tube lights and satellites,
In the sphere of humankind and masterminds.

All those doctorates and PhDs,
Their wisdom and expertise,
Electricity and the printing press,
The telephone and the internet.

Penicillin and the steam engine,
The airplanes and the vaccines,
The transistors and the bicycles,
The refrigerators and the helicopters.

The telescopes and the barcodes,
The paper and the elevator,
The windmill and the jet engine,
The semiconductor and the sewing machine.

All are evidence of our
Innovations and creations,
Our transformation and our evolution.

Non-living beings turned to living beings,
Stone age things turned to robotic wings.

We have come a long way,
But now let's not destroy our planet with
Fossil fuels and industry waste.
Don't build more buildings and cafes.
We need those trees along our ways.

Let's opt for
Electric vehicles and public transportation,
Car sharing and recycling,
Composting and thrift shopping,
Organic farming and rainwater harvesting.

Ups and Downs

A journey of self-discovery,
A tale of unfulfilled love,
The only stoppage I found
Was in the songs I heard.

The rush of the street,
The flow of blood,
Each dripping gene
Was the flower of trust.

Found the belief,
But it's not mine,
It is somebody else's, who has been kind.
Thanks for the beautiful time.

But what if one day
It all seemed gone?
You have to restart
When you are undone.

It all starts fresh,
The shades are still the same,
But the colors are a little plain,
And the process is not the same.

Again, you have come back to me.
The melodies say this to me:
Now that you have come,
Stay here for long
And fix all of yourself
Until you are again gone.

College Years

Scandals and fashionable sandals,
Fests and musical concerts,
Pouts while taking selfies,
And together we are besties.
It's all about, it's all about,
It's all about our college years.

Basketball courts and volleyball shots,
Cafeteria's maggi and korma gravy,
Momos and pani puri,
Xerox copies, chai and coffees.

Freedom and friendships,
Relationships and college trips,
Sneakers and printed T-shirts,
Classrooms and mechanical workshops.

Seniors and their different societies,
Those gatherings and cultural activities,
Coding challenges and cool dance steps,
Hostel life and rooftop parties.
It's all about, it's all about,
It's all about our college years.

Graduation days and bidding farewells,
Last handshakes and stories to tell.
These memories will never fade,
It's all about, it's all about,
It's all about our college years.

Memorable Days

Oh, I just wanna talk about those memorable days,
We used to read books under the shades.
There used to be butterflies above our gaze.
Oh, those were some beautiful and gorgeous days.

Oh, I just wanna talk about those memorable days,
Knitting the sweater while children were playing tag,
The bicycle riding and birds chirping above the lake.
Oh, those were some beautiful and gorgeous days.

Lost

I was running up to the deserted,
Aisle, aisle, aisle.
There was nobody to look for in the entire
Sight, sight, sight.

Y'know, you could be thinking it all in your
Mind, mind, mind,
While you were sitting with your friends in order to
Dine, dine, dine.

Celebs

When you put your arms up,
And flow them like a gel,
When you curve your heels,
And bend them like a sail.

They go up to the streets,
Singing and rhyming all that you say.
You don't know how much they love you,
Cause you are still in the vanity van.

But there are two sides to it,
That people won't understand.
You get cheers and flowers after your performance,
But there's no one to hear you when you're in pain.

Little Do You Know

Little do you know, man,
Little do you know,
The rainbows are lining up,
But never to show,
But never to show.

Little do you know, man,
Little do you know,
The penguins are walking,
But glaciers flow,
But glaciers flow.

Little do you know, man,
Little do you know,
The more you will ripen,
The more you will sow,
The more you will sow.

Phenomena

We have Spiderman,
We have Batman,
And we have Superman,
And also Wonder Woman.

There are galaxies,
And there are star kids.
Don't know where to look,
Ferrari or Mercedes.

We have Harry Potter,
And we have Twilight,
We have Game of Thrones,
And also The Simpsons and Titanic.

Son of an Army Officer

He was the son of an army officer,
He always waited for his dad to come over.
His dad wanted to teach him strength and resilience,
Whenever he came back from the trenches where he had
learnt all his brilliance.

He was still young and tender,
When he had lost his dad,
In a battle of soldiers.
He was just starting to learn,
But now, behind those boulders,

He was soft-spoken, so was bullied,
By his seniors and their friends.
He used to come back home,
Dismantled and drained.

He looked into the picture of his dad,
And wanted him to come out of the frame,
But he realized it's over, and,
He needs to take command.

He became strong and sturdy,
The side his dad always wanted him to aim.

He showed the boys what he is really made of,
The blood of a soldier and the heart of a good human.

20

Adieu

I just wanna shine like
I am new, oh uh, oh uh,
Getting to the situation like
I'm through, oh uh, oh uh.

And your eye color is
Blue, oh uh, oh uh.
It makes me feel like
I'm going through
Déjà vu, oh uh, oh uh.

Just wanna say it's all because of
You, oh uh, oh uh.

Hopefully we
Grew, oh uh, oh uh.
And no more standing in a
Queue, oh uh, oh uh.

And don't have to say to each other
Adieu, oh uh, oh uh.

How Will You Like This

When you keep reaching out
And they don't seem to care,
Hey heart,
How will you like this?

When they promise that
They will remain the same,
But ultimately, they change,
Hey heart,
How will you like this?

I know you love them,
But they are just not the same.
Hey heart,
How will you like this?

When the fear of losing them
Is more than the joy
Of having them,
Hey heart,
How will you like this?

Berries

Strawberries
Sweet old berries.
Strawberries
Could you hold on for something ordinary?

Raspberries
Sweet but tangy,
Raspberries
Will you mind if the opinions are contrary?

Cranberries
Tart and slightly bitter,
Cranberries
Will you ever mind sharing your story?

Blackberries
Taste better in smoothies and jelly,
Blackberries
Would you mind a change that's temporary?

Eternity

Could you stay there for eternity
And guide me through the dynasties?
I can swear that I can fly beneath,
Cause your presence brings me tranquility.

The flowers are growing out of boundaries,
The poets only get to repeat.
We didn't come out of the cave for inequality,
Butterfly wings also hold a lot of creativity.

Keep Going

Even when you have lost,
Even when you can't seem to find hope,
Even when you have no support,
Just keep going and don't stop.

Even when you have to go against the tide,
Even when you have obstacles to fight,
Even when sometimes you might have to end up on the losing side,
Just keep going and don't hide.

This is a City

This is a city,
A globe of equity.
You can be the boss,
You have no loss,
But that's just a cost.

You got to embrace such,
Hold your breath,
Study the rage.
Oh, make this easy,
You have got so much in the city.

Brain, the king of rise,
The only desire,
The thing, the one,
Who pushes you to pretty heights,
The bigger you jump.

Cover uncovers,
Still sober.
Only flowers blossom,
Not a rule.
You cannot stop rain from falling down.
Water rises up nonstop,

It's a verge of control,
At the risk of caliber.

Summer uncommon,
Weather uncertain.
Algorithm only,
Song reaches shape.
No step calls it a stop,
Only the sky turns black and light.

How Much Can You Love Yourself

There is no limit, there is no end line.
How much can you love yourself
When you remain serene and don't hurt yourself?
How much can you love yourself?

You see the wrong side but decide otherwise.
How much can you love yourself
When you no longer need others to validate?
How much can you love yourself?

You have forgiven and moved on.
How much can you love yourself?
You embraced reality to its best.
How much can you love yourself?

When you know perfection's not the way,
How much can you love yourself?
When guilt no longer leads your day,
How much can you love yourself?

The Expedition

This is going to be my last expedition.
I am retiring from next year,
So while I am out there clicking photographs, crystal and clear,
I know I will remember all that brought me here.

At eighteen, I received my first camera.
Back then, I had started this journey.
I photographed jaguars beneath the dense canopy.
I trekked through the icy landscapes of the Arctic,
Just to spend a day full of polar bears that looked fantastic.

In summers, I captured the antics of sea otters in the forests of Alaska,
And the movements of manta rays in the warm waters of the Maldives.
In winters, I captured Elk against the backdrop of snow-covered peaks,
And also the snow hare, as through the white silence it streaks.

For my last expedition I chose the Galápagos Islands.
I saw penguins darting through the water,

And flamingos with their vibrant pink feathers.
For one last time, I clicked a picture
and heard the shutter.
I realized it's not about the perfect shot.
It is about understanding the essence of life in the wild
And experiencing nature's purest moments
As nature's beauty is always eternally sought.

www.ingramcontent.com/pod-product-compliance
Lightning Source LLC
LaVergne TN
LVHW010836200726
843508LV00012B/2619